HANSARD

by Simon Woods

USE OF COPYRIGHTED MUSIC

USE OF COPYRIGHTED THIRD-PARTY MATERIALS

IMPORTANT BILLING AND CREDIT REQUIREMENTS

FIRST PERFORMANCE

Hansard was first performed at The National Theatre on 22 August 2019. The cast was as follows:

DIANA	LINDSAY DUNCAN
ROBIN	ALEX JENNINGS
DIRECTOR	SIMON GODWIN
MOVEMENT DIRECTOR	SHELLEY MAXWELL
SET AND COSTUME DESIGNER	HILDEGARD BECHTLER
LIGHTING DESIGNER	JACKIE SHEMESH
SOUND DESIGNER	CHRISTOPHER SHUTT
ASSOCIATE DIRECTOR	EMILY BURNS
COMPANY VOICE WORK	JEANNETTE NELSON
VIDEO CONTENT	ISSAC MADGE
MUSIC	MICHAEL BRUCE

AUTHOR'S NOTE

There are stage directions in the text that correspond to Hildegard Bechtler's design for the original production. They suggest that the action all takes place in one room and they demand an Aga, curtains, cupboards and so on. Please feel free to ignore them.

The only thing that feels important is that the characters come and go in some way, so that each of them has moments alone on stage.

If it's practical, then two or more distinct spaces might be ideal. I often had the feeling as I was writing that conversations were happening between rooms – that there was an apartness to their proximity.

The only other thing to say about the design is that the clutter under the table is important. The pulling out of boxes and bags and *stuff* acts both as a kind of scene change and a visual metaphor. As does tidying away at the end. I suppose this could be achieved with a cupboard instead.

The final thing to say is that variety of tone and pace and pitch feel like the key to the play. As important as sharpness of the dialogue and the ferocity of the emotions, and the moments of stillness and silence and tenderness. It should feel like a continual game of approach and retreat, as they test each others limits, and their own.

Simon Woods, June 2020

CHARACTERS

It doesn't really matter how old they are. Somewhere between fifty and seventy, I imagine. I've taken out most of the dates from their back story so that age isn't an issue. The important thing is that you should believe that they once adored each other, and that it might be possible again.

ROBIN – has the almost hysterical verbal energy of a man who has never confronted his feelings. He speaks in a series of verbal jack-in-a-box escapes from emotional intimacy or truthfulness. There has to be a relish and a verbal exuberance to him.

DIANA – is dazzling. She ought to have been something wonderful. But somehow, unbearably, here she is…

(Saturday 27th May, 1988.)

(Some time after eleven o'clock. It's a sunny morning, but the curtains are still closed.)

(We are in a country house in Oxfordshire. Georgian. Good bones, but not large.)

(Some suggestion of the reality of the building feels as though it might be useful: this is a house with a porch full of battered Barbours, wellies, sleeveless puffers, an assortment of walking sticks. An AGA. It's a house with good furniture. Cupboards full of inherited china.)

(If a naturalistic set feels right, then there should be something that prevents it from feeling like a home, though. No photographs anywhere, none of the cheerful carnage of a family house. Not quite enough furniture, perhaps?)

(Perhaps we glimpse what is beyond the house? The gold and green of the Cotswolds? Some gesture of the garden? Of the trees that surround the building?)

(Perhaps not. Perhaps none of this.)

(The only thing that's indispensable is a long dining table that is used for storage rather than entertaining. There should be stuff crammed underneath it, spilling out onto the chairs around it: an ancient toy car, a lamp, an old cine projector, lots of plastic bags... and then boxes – as many as possible, and of all different shapes and sizes.)

(Something about the way things are arranged on top of the table must show us that this set up is permanent. There's an Anglepoise lamp, perhaps even more than one, bent over some trays of puzzle pieces. Piles of books and of post. A tablecloth that looks as though it's been in place for years.)

(All this belongs to **DIANA** *and* **ROBIN HESKETH***. Both are in late middle age.)*

(If **DIANA** *had her ambitions nurtured and her intelligence taken seriously, she would have been a successful publisher. Or maybe a broadcaster in the Joan Bakewell mode. She probably had a book in her too, though she never found it. Certainly she's too bright to have lead the life she has. The result is a complex combination of capability and regret. Part sumptuous intelligence, part brittle self-loathing.)*

(ROBIN*'s ambitions, on the other hand, have always been taken seriously. Every door he has ever encountered has been held open for him. Eton, Oxford, the bar, Parliament. He hardly even had to learn to push. Now a Conservative MP and junior minister in Margaret Thatcher's recently re-elected government, he has the absolute, unquestioning self-confidence of the successful public-school-educated Englishman. He is patrician without being pompous. Powerful without having to demonstrate his power. Privileged without being aware of it. He is also charming.)*

(When the play begins, he is just returning home from an overnight trip to Leeds, where he appeared, the night before, on Any Questions.*)*

(As **ROBIN** *enters, he is humming snatches of "Happy Birthday" to himself. Cheerfully, he puts his things down. Suddenly he catches sight of something out through the window. Horror-struck.)*

ROBIN. Oh no!

(Looking out into the garden / the audience.)

Not again.

LEAVE ME ALONE!

DIANA. They never will, you know.

(ROBIN. *hasn't been aware of* **DIANA***'s presence until now and ideally nor have we.)*

ROBIN. Diana?

DIANA. 'Fraid so, darling.

ROBIN. *(exaggerated amazement)* My God, she's still alive!

(This makes **DIANA** *laugh.)*

DIANA. Still breathing away.

ROBIN. Well done you –

DIANA. Still hauling my carcass round the kitchen.

ROBIN. Ah, but what a carcass it is. Look at that, ladies and gentlemen! She's still got it –

DIANA. Do I really?

ROBIN. Age shall not weary her, nor the years condemn...

(ROBIN *has put down his bags and is heading back towards the hall.)*

DIANA. There we are.

Miss Havisham, eat your heart out.

ROBIN. *(offstage)* Miss what?

DIANA. Never mind.

That's the hope, though, is it? Get back one weekend and find me face down in the catmint. Drowned in the bath. I can see it must be terribly disappointing.

ROBIN. *(offstage)* I'm spending a penny –

DIANA. Especially when one thinks of the poor old health service.

ROBIN. *(offstage)* I can't hear –

DIANA. Because you're turning them away in droves, aren't you? They're dying in the corridors, and I can't even catch a bit of shingles.

You know what I blame?

ROBIN. *(offstage)* Me, I imagine.

DIANA. The Cotswolds. Look at them. The cow parsley frothing along the hedgerows, the scent of freshly cut hay. Christ, one could go on forever.

(**ROBIN.** *re-enters*).

You know what we need? If you're ever going to get rid of me. A dual carriage way.

ROBIN. An –

DIANA. A road. Steady stream of heavy goods vehicles. Right down the middle of the valley.

(**ROBIN** *is looking at* **DIANA.**, *trying to work out what's going on.*)

You could make it happen, couldn't you? It's your constituency.

ROBIN. I missed the beginning.

DIANA. Open up the ozone layer –

ROBIN. Are you alright?

DIANA. I'm thriving, Robin. This is it!

ROBIN. You're not dressed –

DIANA. The odd self-inflicted fracture aside, I'm in relentlessly good health –

ROBIN. It's after eleven.

DIANA. No getting rid of me –

ROBIN. And you know what day it is –

DIANA. I suppose there's always smoking.

ROBIN. I'm sorry?

(**ROBIN.** *gives up and goes to open the curtains.*)

DIANA. How many do you think one would have to get through a day to give oneself a really good shot at cancer –

ROBIN. Oh for goodness sake!

DIANA. Ten do you think? Twenty?

ROBIN. Don't be disgusting –

DIANA. No, you're right – course you are. (*As though full of remorse*) I'm sorry.

ROBIN. Anyway –

DIANA. Because it's such an unattractive way to go, isn't it? All that hair tufting out in the shower. There we are.

(Dazzling smile.)

Vanity prevails yet again.

ROBIN. Are you going to be like this all day?

DIANA. Do you know? I think I am –

ROBIN. Oh good... excellent.

*(Suddenly **ROBIN** is walking purposefully towards **DIANA**, peering right at her.)*

DIANA. But then you didn't think you'd get away with it, did you?

ROBIN. Sorry?

DIANA. I mean, the news does reach us out here in the provinces – what is it?

*(**ROBIN** is looking at **DIANA**'s face.)*

ROBIN. I'm just...

*(**DIANA**'s hand instinctively goes to her cheek –)*

DIANA. What?

ROBIN. No, it's no good.

DIANA. What are you doing?

ROBIN. I was trying to remember why I married you.

*(Despite herself, this makes **DIANA** laugh. In this moment in which her guard comes down, **ROBIN** approaches.)*

And why I still come back to you like this. That's the real question. Week after week. Flogging my way down the motorway. Why do I put myself through it?

DIANA. Oh I don't know, Robin.

Guilt, I imagine –

ROBIN. Sorry?

DIANA. Well it's either that or the garden –

ROBIN. Oh *don't.*

DIANA. What?

ROBIN. It's unbearable –

DIANA. The guilt?

ROBIN. The garden.

>   *(Off Diana's quizzical look.)*

>   Don't tell me you haven't noticed?

DIANA. Noticed?

>   The damage! Look at it!

>   Oh the *damage* –

ROBIN. Again –

DIANA. No I did see that – of course I did. I'm so sorry.

>   *(**DIANA** has joined **ROBIN** at the window.)*

>   Because it's heart-breaking –

ROBIN. Well I think so –

DIANA. To see it in that sort of state –

ROBIN. Exactly –

DIANA. Ravaged like that –

ROBIN. Yes –

DIANA. Decimated –

ROBIN. I know –

DIANA. Whole country in tatters –

ROBIN. What? –

DIANA. And yet for some extraordinary reason they all keep voting
Conservative.

>   *(Dazzling smile.)*

What's wrong with them? Because you think they'd learn, wouldn't you? At some point?

ROBIN. Ha ha.

DIANA. And I'm always telling them not to vote for you –

ROBIN. Oh are you –

DIANA. I wander the streets of Witney, telling them –

ROBIN. Oh good –

DIANA. I accost them in the supermarket –

ROBIN. I'm so pleased –

DIANA. If you'd just stop and look – this is what I say as I totter the fruit and veg aisle – you'll notice that the natural party of government is in fact unbelievably bad at it. Hopeless! One catastrophic act of national self-sabotage after another –

ROBIN. Yes I was talking about the garden –

DIANA. And yet like a battered wife they keep coming back to you –

ROBIN. Oh do shut up, Diana –

DIANA. I tell you, it's the great mystery of our time. The insatiable desire of the people of this country to be fucked by an Old Etonian –

ROBIN. I was talking about the fox.

DIANA. I'm sorry?

ROBIN. As you know perfectly well. Look at my poor lawn.

DIANA. Oh I *see* –

ROBIN. It's like the Somme out there –

DIANA. *(all innocence)* Oh I can't bear it, Robin – how embarrassing – because I thought you were talking about the country, you see –

ROBIN. Yes alright –

DIANA. This blessed plot –

ROBIN. Yes –

DIANA. This England –

ROBIN. Oh don't start up again! Not sure I can take any more.

DIANA. Go on – I can have one more go –

ROBIN. No you can't!

DIANA. No, alright. *(Brightly)* Wasn't bad though, was it? This stage in the day.

ROBIN. It was alright.

DIANA. Without a warm up.

ROBIN. It was fine.

DIANA. Just a sort of... standing jump.

(Dazzling smile.)

ROBIN. Sorry?

DIANA. Isn't that what it was called? No run up. Both feet together and they just hurled themselves out into the sandpit.

ROBIN. I don't –

DIANA. Of course you do. The standing jump, Robin. Oh come on – the moments of sporting triumph in our family have been so few and far between, you can't possibly have forgotten. That final sports day at *The Dragon*. The banks of the Cherwell, the distant sound of cricket balls, the car parks full of Volvos –

ROBIN. What are you doing?

DIANA. Nostlagia, darling. Well don't give me that look – it's more or less the entire electoral strategy of the Tory Party...

*(**ROBIN.** has had enough. He heads off upstage to do something – fill the kettle? Put it onto the hot side of the AGA?)*

And he won a rosette! Didn't he? Come on, darling, make an effort –

ROBIN. I suppose there's always AIDS.

DIANA. I'm sorry?

ROBIN. What do you think?

DIANA. AIDS?

ROBIN. Only you said you wanted to catch something.

> (**ROBIN.** *does Diana's dazzling smile.*)

In the absence of an A road. And of course it's *terribly* infectious. Trouble with cancer, it's so hit and miss.

DIANA. Yes alright –

ROBIN. Go on – a bit of intravenous drug use. Some unprotected sex. You might even enjoy it. And you know what? *(Gasps – really thrilled with this idea – hand on her arm if he's close enough)* I bet we could get you a visit from Lady Di!

DIANA. Sorry?

ROBIN. Because she's mad about them! Isn't she! Can't keep her out of the AIDS wards. So many photographers in there, the nurses can hardly get at the patients.

DIANA. Yes alright –

ROBIN. Bring some press along – it could be your big moment! I'm seeing you on the front page of all the papers. And God knows you deserve it, my darling. You've waited in the wings for long enough!

DIANA. Is that what I've been doing –

ROBIN. All these years you've been there in the background, cheering me on. The torrents of support.

DIANA. Ha –

ROBIN. It's your turn to shine.

DIANA. Thank you, darling –

ROBIN. No it's a pleasure. It really is. I shall drive you into Cirencester after lunch –

> (**ROBIN** *turns to head back to the front door, where he has left his bags.*)

DIANA. You're too kind, Robin.

ROBIN. *(In the doorway upstage, centre, taking the compliment with a kind of pained sincerity)* Well I am.

DIANA. Too thoughtful –

ROBIN. No, it's a failing. It really is.

(**ROBIN**'s *left the room by now*).

It's why the great offices of state have eluded me.

(**DIANA** *is alone on stage.*)

DIANA. I thought they'd eluded you because you didn't have the right sort of wife.

ROBIN. *(offstage)* What?

DIANA. That's what you normally imply.

ROBIN. *(reappearing)* My dear girl, I'd never *dream* of implying that –

DIANA. Poor old Robin. That's what they all think, isn't it? Lumbered with that frightful left wing woman –

ROBIN. Nobody thinks that.

DIANA. Of course they do.

ROBIN. No, darling, I promise you. They don't think you're left wing. They think you're highly strung.

DIANA. Oh fuck off –

(**ROBIN.** *exits back again.*)

(Beat.)

And anyway, I'm not highly strung. I'm profoundly unhappy.

ROBIN. *(offstage)* What did you say?

Beat.

(offstage) I didn't hear.

DIANA. It doesn't matter.

*(Silence. **DIANA.**, alone.)*

(We should feel that there is something more she might say. She doesn't.)

*(**ROBIN** re-enters carrying two plastic bags and his ministerial red box.)*

ROBIN. *(offstage)* You know what I was trying to remember in the car.

*(**ROBIN.** reappears in the central doorway.)*

Who was it that had his brain preserved?

*(**ROBIN** has a huge pile of newspapers in his arms.)*

Couldn't bear the thought that when he died, all the wonders of his mind were just going to evaporate. So he had it pickled. Do you remember? It was one of the philosophers –

DIANA. *(quietly, almost to herself)* Bentham –

ROBIN. We saw it at the fundraiser. UCL –

DIANA. *(louder)* Bentham.

ROBIN. That's it. Well done, old girl –

DIANA. All still there, you see –

ROBIN. I was thinking it's not a bad response, is it? Set oneself in aspic. Live on in the larder.

*(**ROBIN** flops the papers down on the table.)*

Because what will one leave behind otherwise? Really? In the final reckoning?

DIANA. Oh I don't know…a deregulated financial services industry –

ROBIN. What's that?

DIANA. A less equal society –

ROBIN. I mean it!

DIANA. So do I –

ROBIN. A bag of one's clothes trundling down to the charity shop. Is that the best we can hope for? One may be dead, but one's suits will still be worn.

DIANA. Who needs God when you've got Sue Ryder.

ROBIN. There's always Hansard, I suppose. That's some consolation. That one's been transcribed. Live on in the library of the House of Commons. Throw in an obituary of some sort, presumably. Good chap. Never quite fulfilled his early promise.

(**ROBIN** *is walking towards the door now.*)

DIANA. You know who I blame?

ROBIN. Ted Heath? Me too, darling. Frightful man.

(**ROBIN.** *exits very briefly again to collect his post, but it doesn't stop the flow of the dialogue, they just speak louder when he is offstage.*)

Colonel Nasser possibly –

DIANA. I mean your lawn. The fox.

ROBIN. Oh yes?

DIANA. I blame your mother.

ROBIN. *(offstage)* Mummy?

DIANA. All her fault –

ROBIN. *(in the doorway, huge pile of post in his hands)* Diana, my mother's been dead since 1979. I'm not sure you can pin this one on her. Oh my God – unless you've had her moved?

DIANA. What?

ROBIN. You have! You've had her dug up and reburied in the garden. No wonder they're going beserk –

DIANA. I mean because she wore one.

You remember. Awful thing with its face still on. Whiskers. Glass eyes. Slung over one shoulder –

ROBIN. Oh I see –

DIANA. Petrified Tom when he was small –

ROBIN. And you think they're getting their revenge do you? Been looking for me ever since –

DIANA. That's it –

ROBIN. Sniffing their way through the home counties?

DIANA. Well come on – isn't that always the story in our family?

ROBIN. What?

DIANA. The sins of the parents, Robin. Something rotten in the state of Lechlade. They've worked out that if you really want to upset a middle-aged Englishman of slender emotional means, it's his lawn you want to go for. It's his little wicket.

(**ROBIN** *stops doing his post for a moment and looks up at* **DIANA.***)*

ROBIN. Diana?

DIANA. Yes.

ROBIN. What are you doing?

DIANA. I'm discussing the state of the garden.

ROBIN. You're not dressed.

DIANA. I'm thinking it must be a metaphor for something. Mustn't it? This little patch of ground. Torn to shreds like that. Family life, do you think? State of our marriage –

ROBIN. Well I wish they'd leave my analogy alone, that's all I know. *(Enjoying himself)* Go on – get the fuck off my metaphor!

(**ROBIN.** *laughs. It subsides into a kind of melancholy.*)

What *do* you think it wants? In all seriousness. What do you think it's hoping to find?

DIANA. I honestly don't know, Robin.

(*Beat.* **DIANA** *can't resist.*)

Roman coins, do you think?

ROBIN. You don't care at all, do you?

(**ROBIN** *looks at* **DIANA.** *He is suddenly struck by a terribly thought.*)

Oh my God, you're probably feeding them!

(*This makes* **DIANA.** *laugh.*)

I don't know why you're laughing. Because it was a labour of enormous love, making that lawn –

DIANA. I know it was –

ROBIN. And if you remember what it was like when we first got here. Great lumpy patch of field –

DIANA. No I do remember –

ROBIN. And all the hours I spent out there with the roller. Back and forth, week after week.

DIANA. Yes I'm agreeing with you –

ROBIN. And every few hours I'd come in and tell you I was ready for an inspection.

(Beat. This is a moment of tenderness, of approach.)

And you'd wander out in your bare feet. Babe in arms. Very serious. I've found a lump you'd say. Point at it with your big toe. More rolling required.

(This makes **DIANA** *look over at* **ROBIN***. The flicker of something soft between them. A beat.)*

DIANA. *(quietly)* Yes, alright.

ROBIN. There we are, you see! You never believe me, but we were.

DIANA. Were what?

ROBIN. Happy.

DIANA. Happy? No, darling, you're getting confused. That was the other one.

ROBIN. The other what?

DIANA. The first Mrs De Winter.

Oh Lord, you haven't forgotten her as well? *(Then, as though speaking to an extremely elderly relative)* Susannah, she was called –

ROBIN. Oh don't.

DIANA. Lipstick. Lot of blonde hair –

ROBIN. She was a very a nice woman.

DIANA. I know she was –

ROBIN. To whom I behaved extremely badly.

DIANA. Well I know that too...

ROBIN. What do you mean?

DIANA. What do I...

(under her breath) Oh dear this is awkward.

(elderly relative again) I was the girl in the hotel, Robin! I was the bit on the side –

ROBIN. *(laughs, playing along – mock incredulous)* No!

DIANA. I know! Can you bear it. It was me, clattering against the head board. Bum in the air!

ROBIN. Yes alright –

DIANA. Bun in the oven. Well don't do that face. That was the high point of it all. The two star hotels. The Berni Inns.

(Gorgeous smile.)

It's been down hill ever since...

*(**DIANA** moves to exit, but **ROBIN** stops her at the door with a shift in tone:)*

ROBIN. *(tender)* We did have fun, I think. At the beginning. Didn't we? Made each other laugh.

DIANA. *(sincere, quiet)* Yes.

ROBIN. Those terrible suppers. And my God, you were beautiful.

*(**DIANA.** smiles at **ROBIN.**. A kind of tenderness.)*

DIANA. I was desperately in love with you, Robin.

ROBIN. Oh well –

DIANA. And I felt lucky. I did. That you'd chosen me.

(jaunty) And the rest, as they say, is tragedy.

ROBIN. I don't think that's exactly what they say.

DIANA. No? Then they should come and spend the weekend with us.

(**DIANA** *exits, laughing.*)

(*We should see* **ROBIN** *relax. He swaps his shoes for a more comfortable pair? He takes off his tie? We should feel that he's letting his guard down.*)

(**DIANA** *returns and stands in the doorway upstage. She has a pot plant with her – a geranium, I imagine, which she will put on the table when it feels right. She speaks with the kind of off-hand nonchalance.*)

DIANA. Is that still the drill, by the way?

ROBIN. What?

DIANA. A regional hotel.

Beat.

ROBIN. What do you mean?

DIANA. No I remember the logic: because you were never going to run into anyone who mattered in Swindon. Wasn't that right? Everyone you knew either lived in London or they lived in the country. You might as well be in Azerbaijan.

ROBIN. Swindon?

DIANA. Or wherever it is, I don't know. Wolverhampton? Because there's something unutterably lower-middle class about a town, isn't there? A minor city.

ROBIN. I don't understand.

DIANA. I remember when I told you my parents lived in Reigate, you were horrified. And I didn't even know it was embarrassing! That was the worst thing. Nobody had ever told us. We were laboring under the tragic misapprehension that Reigate was rather smart –

ROBIN. I'm not –

DIANA. I mean, we'd made it out of Dorking.

ROBIN. What are you talking about, Diana?

DIANA. *(lightly)* Well I'm talking about your Wednesdays.

ROBIN. My Wednesdays?

DIANA. Oh no don't do coy, Robin. Not sure I can bear it –

ROBIN. I'm genuinely not with you.

DIANA. Yes that's rather my point, funnily enough.

(**DIANA** *laughs. She has returned to the table with a plastic bin. She is not looking at* **ROBIN**.)

Look at you. I see that swagger in your step.

ROBIN. Swagger?

DIANA. Swish in your tail. Something must have set that off. Can't just be the damage you're inflicting on the most vulnerable in society.

(*Dazzling smile. During the following dialogue she will pluck the dead heads and the brown leaves from the geranium and throw them into the bin.*)

ROBIN. No you're getting muddled, darling. Because I haven't risked a swagger in years.

DIANA. Sorry?

ROBIN. I tell you, with a lumber spine like mine – with discs as herniated as these... And as for a swish! My God—

DIANA. No there's no need to panic.

ROBIN. I'm not panicking –

DIANA. Honestly, the squandering of my affections is the least of our worries –

ROBIN. Your affections?

DIANA. In the grand scheme of things –

ROBIN. Diana Hesketh, I haven't been on the receiving end of your affections since some time during the Falklands.

DIANA. Oh I see...that's the line, is it? Poor old Robin –

ROBIN. No –

DIANA. Although I'm not sure you *can* pin that one on me, actually. Dereliction of wifely duty. If you recall what happened the last time I essayed that particular peak?

ROBIN. When?

DIANA. If I remember rightly, I got hold of the remote control, turned off *Newsnight* and edged my way with what I thought was no small amount of allure over to your side of the bed.

ROBIN. Allure!

DIANA. You had a peer under the duvet. "You've got no clothes on", you said.

I said *(seductive:)* I know.

Aghast, that's how you looked –

ROBIN. Oh come on –

DIANA. You did. You looked at me and you said, you're not getting Alzheimer's, are you?

ROBIN. *(laughing, then adopting lawyerly voice)* Forcing myself for a moment to recall the details of the night in question.

DIANA. *(eye-rolling)* Oh no –

ROBIN. Forcing myself, your honour, to revisit the whole painful episode, I feel bound to say that I was incapacitated. I was overcome –

DIANA. Overcome, were you?

ROBIN. To state the case for the defence, it was the gin fumes wot did it!

DIANA. Oh don't start that up –

ROBIN. I'm afraid it's like being down wind of the bottle bank when my wife clambers into bed –

DIANA. Yes, alright –

ROBIN. That's the truth, your worship. I'm afraid this *allure* smells like a marquee on the morning after a wedding – speaking of which!

DIANA. What?

ROBIN. Holy shit –

DIANA. What?

*(**ROBIN** is holding an empty gin bottle aloft.)*

ROBIN. My darling, your liver is a thing of wonder. My God!

*(**ROBIN** is looking at the spirit bottles.)*

Dennis Thatcher has nothing on you.

DIANA. Look on my works, ye mighty, and despair.

*(This makes **ROBIN** laugh.)*

ROBIN. And I thought you said you didn't need to drink when I wasn't here.

DIANA. Sometimes just the thought of you is enough.

*(**ROBIN.** is holding the empty bottles in his hand.)*

ROBIN. Extraordinary. I shall have to donate it somewhere when you die. One of the wonders of medical science. I shall get a little plaque made. Here lies the liver of Diana Hesketh, it will say. *Ginorously* donated –

*(**ROBIN.** drops one of them into the bin, the one **DIANA.** has brought over for the deadheading.)*

DIANA. You're still going are you –

*(**ROBIN.** is enjoying himself, now, clanking another bottle into **DIANA.**'s bin as he talks.)*

ROBIN. I could do an endowment to go with it –

DIANA. Oh my God you are –

ROBIN. One for the lush fund, I shall call it –

DIANA. *(cupping her hands round her mouth and shouting)* Yes I think you've done that now –

ROBIN. Oh go on. I can have one more bash –

DIANA. No you can't –

ROBIN. Not even –

DIANA. No.

(*Beat.*)

ROBIN. No alright. (*Brightly*) Wasn't bad, though, was it?

DIANA. It was fine.

ROBIN. Without a run up.

DIANA. (*leaping on this*) Sorry?

ROBIN. This stage in the day –

DIANA. (*triumphant*) That's it!

ROBIN. That's what?

DIANA. Oh I'm *so* pleased!

ROBIN. What are you doing?

DIANA. You do remember the standing jump!

ROBIN. (*caught on the hop*) I didn't –

DIANA. It *was* called the standing jump, wasn't it? I'm not making that up? Both feet together and they just threw themselves out into the sandpit. Like a frog in a nature documentary –

But you know what?

(*Suddenly she is moving across to the huge long table.* **ROBIN** *is watching her.*)

ROBIN. What are you doing now?

DIANA. We had a cine film of it –

ROBIN. Sorry?

DIANA. Didn't we?

(*She is lifting up the table cloth to reveal that the space beneath is crammed with stuff.*)

We did! Prize-giving ceremony. The whole thing. You remember? Well of course you do. You always loved those sports days.

*(Looking for the box of old cine films, **DIANA** pulls several other boxes out from under the table.)*

You used to get quite misty-eyed about them, didn't you? But then it *was* rather moving. All those boys in their cricket whites. The ruling class being formed before one's very eyes –

ROBIN. I'm not sure I'm necessarily in the mood for this –

DIANA. Oh go on, Robin. It's been years since we got these out. Far too long.

*(**DIANA**'s peering into the box.)*

Now, let's see, what have we got?

(She has to read the labels on each cine reel as she takes them out of the box.)

(She puts the rejected reels onto the table as she goes.)

France. Norfolk. Norfolk. Wedding! Ha. We could try that later. World's most pregnant bride. Your parents looking like they were sucking on a lemon.

*(**DIANA** is facing away from **ROBIN** He pulls a face or snarls silently at her or mimes strangling her or shooting himself or whatever gesture feels right. Without looking round, **DIANA** knows what he's doing.)*

Oh don't be like that, darling. I kept thinking that this week, you know. As I watched it all unfold. *(Light)* That it's been a sort of catastrophe. This failure to look back.

ROBIN. Watched what unfold?

DIANA. There we go!

*(**DIANA.**'s found the reel. She is holding the reel away from her to read what the rest of the label says.)*

Oh and look – it's on the same reel as that Hustings you did in Wallingford, so you'll enjoy that at least. Now, listen, I'll find the projector, you close the curtains.

*(**ROBIN** does not move.)*

Wallingford. Perils of an enlarged common market if I remember rightly?

ROBIN. What are you doing, Diana?

*(The projector is tucked away on the far side of the table. To get to it, **DIANA** has to shunt the table out from the wall.)*

DIANA. Well you know what they say: if you don't learn your history then you're doomed to repeat it.

Who did say that? Was it Ghandi? Sounds like Ghandi. Or Norman Lamont.

*(**DIANA.**'s managed to shunt the table across a little with her hip.)*

ROBIN. You've been cooped up all week, have you?

DIANA. Sorry?

ROBIN. Because this is quite a performance.

DIANA. Oh no, Robin, no. I've had a rather busy week actually –

ROBIN. Busy?

DIANA. One way and another –

ROBIN. Good Lord, you haven't been moving the cushions round on the sofa again have you?

*(**DIANA.**'s found the projector now. She's dragging it out round the front of the table.)*

DIANA. Here it is –

ROBIN. You're not really doing this –

DIANA. Oh go on. You might even enjoy it. Because I was still in my adoring phase then, wasn't I? Nodding up at you in all those village halls, clapping at all the right moments –

ROBIN. There was an adoring phase, was there?

DIANA. I was very good at the beginning. All those headscarves I wore. The twin sets. The casual racism.

*(**DIANA.** heaves the projector up onto the table.)*

Best supporting wife. That's what I was going for.

ROBIN. Although you didn't actually vote for me, did you?

DIANA. Of course I did –

ROBIN. No go on – you can tell me – in the privacy of the booth.

DIANA. I kept on voting for you for years, Robin.

(**DIANA.** *gives him a lovely smile.*)

But then in my defence, you do all *look* like you know what you're doing.

ROBIN. Sorry?

(**DIANA.** *is holding the projector's cable in her hand and wondering which socket she can plug it into.*)

DIANA. That's the trouble with the British class system, isn't it? So easy to mistake an expensive education for an actual understanding of the world.

(**DIANA.** *starts to cross over to the kitchen to find the extension lead.*)

ROBIN. Please.

(**DIANA.** *is rummaging around in a cupboard.* **ROBIN.** *watches her.*)

I don't ask for much. But I'm asking you not to do this. The Scotts'll be here in an hour. I'd like us to be able to have a nice day with them.

DIANA. A nice day?

ROBIN. I'm not expecting the full Norma Major. I'm thinking more a sort of Tintern Abbey sort of feel. We may be ruined but we're still standing. What do you think? Try not to get downwind of the sherry too early on in proceedings?

DIANA. I imagine the sherry might help –

ROBIN. Try not to look as though you disagree with me *every* time I open my mouth.

(**DIANA.** *has found what she was looking for. It is a long wind-up extension lead. She looks at him.*)

DIANA. Honestly? I don't think I could do it –

ROBIN. No need to listen to what I was saying. Just nod along occasionally. That's how my mother dealt with my father, wasn't it? "Yes, darling", she said, every three or four minutes. "Quite right" – little nod –

DIANA. And that's what you'd like us to aim for, is it? Your parents?

ROBIN. Well it worked pretty well for them.

DIANA. Ha!

ROBIN. You laugh, but they were married for sixty years. Must have got something right.

(*This stops* **DIANA** *still. She turns slowly to look at* **ROBIN.**)

DIANA. Oh my God.

ROBIN. What?

DIANA. You're not joking, are you?

ROBIN. Why? I think they had a pretty successful marriage.

(*Beat.*)

DIANA. Robin, your father had a mistress and two children in Hemel Hempstead.

ROBIN. Oh *that* –

DIANA. He had an entire second life running in parallel.

ROBIN. Of course he didn't. Honestly.

DIANA. What would you call them, then?

(*Beat.*)

ROBIN. Well it was a different time.

DIANA. Ha.

ROBIN. The point is it worked for them.

DIANA. No, darling, it worked for *him*. I realise that's an incredibly nuanced distinction.

(**DIANA** *plugs the extension lead into the wall. She begins to unspools it across the stage towards the projector.*)

ROBIN. *(quietly, turned away from* **DIANA***)* They were happier than we are.

DIANA. I'm sorry?

ROBIN. It doesn't matter –

DIANA. You don't think your mother was happy?

ROBIN. Well of course I do.

(**DIANA** *stares at* **ROBIN** *in wonder.*)

What?

DIANA. Are *all* other human beings an impenetrable mystery to you? Or is it just women?

ROBIN. I don't –

DIANA. Robin, your mother was the most furiously unhappy person I've ever met.

ROBIN. Oh don't be ridiculous –

DIANA. But then I suppose she had been ritually humiliated by her husband over a period of twenty years –

ROBIN. No, you never understood my parents.

DIANA. Ha.

ROBIN. But then, you think everyone is like you. That's the trouble –

DIANA. Like me?

ROBIN. Psychological.

DIANA. Ha!

ROBIN. Truth is, it's perfectly possible not to get bogged down in all that.

DIANA. *(amused)* Yes it's called repression, darling.

ROBIN. No it's called getting on with one's life. Everyone has problems, Diana. Everyone. Not everybody chooses to wallow in them like you.

This makes **DIANA.** *pull up and turn.*

DIANA. Oh is that right?

ROBIN. *(slightly regretting having said that)* Life's not about the hand you're dealt. It's about how you choose to play that hand.

(**DIANA.** *smiles. There is something frightening and dangerous about her suddenly.)*

DIANA. Course it is –

ROBIN. In my experience, the trick is to do something. Doesn't even really matter what it is. Just pick something and do it to the best of your ability. Contribute to something larger than oneself. Look outward. You think I'm being obtuse, but I'm not. I've often thought that about you.

DIANA. Sorry?

ROBIN. That it would have been easier if you'd had something else to focus on. Work.

(She looks at him with a sudden white hot rage.)

DIANA. Me?

ROBIN. I don't think I'm wrong, you know –

DIANA. You're saying you think it would have been easier for me if I'd worked?

ROBIN. Well I do.

DIANA. Amazing.

ROBIN. What?

DIANA. You made me stop working, Robin.

ROBIN. What do you mean?

DIANA. You took my work away from me.

ROBIN. No I didn't –

(**DIANA** *laughs in a kind of bewildered disbelief and frustration.*)

DIANA. You told me it was frightfully emabarrassing for an MP's wife to be scurrying around some other man's office. You told me a child needed its mother and that we didn't need my salary and you made me feel my whole career was a joke.

ROBIN. Oh come on. You didn't have a career!

(*Savage laugh from* **DIANA.**)

Well you didn't. You were a pretty girl in a publishing house.

(*Rather than saying anything,* **DIANA** *turns back to the projector.*)

DIANA. I'll just leave that hanging in the air, I think...

ROBIN. What I meant was that you can contribute a lot as an MP's wife.

DIANA. Ah –

ROBIN. If you'd thrown yourself into it. It can be a partnership –

DIANA. No, you know what I should do!

ROBIN. What?

DIANA. I should open a cinema! That's the answer! Fire up the projector!

(**DIANA** *flicks on the switch over on the kitchen side of the stage and the projector on the other side of the stage flares into life.*)

ROBIN. Oh for Christ's sake!

DIANA. Well you said it – I need *something* to keep me cheerful –

ROBIN. STOP IT.

(**ROBIN.** *switches it off at the projector itself.*)

Honestly. You're behaving appallingly this morning. Wretched woman.

And look at this mess you've made. Honestly.

Put it all back in the box.

(**DIANA** *turns to him, a kind of awful half smile.*)

DIANA. *Really?*

ROBIN. What?

DIANA. I mean I know you don't believe in Freud, but...

(*Beat.*)

ROBIN. I don't have to come back, you know.

DIANA. Sorry?

ROBIN. People ask me why I do. Did you know that? All the time, people ask me.

DIANA. And what do you say?

ROBIN. Pity. Mainly.

DIANA. Ha!

(*Beat – sudden realisation.*)

Oh my God, you don't really think you're doing this for my sake, do you? Now that really is a bad joke.

(**DIANA** *laughs.*)

You think I sit here, longing for the weekend, do you?

ROBIN. No –

DIANA. Desperately listening for the sound of your car on the gravel?

ROBIN. No –

DIANA. You think I want you to come back?

ROBIN. Honestly? I don't know what you want, Diana. I have no idea.

DIANA. No.

ROBIN. But I know what I want. Normal day. Nice lunch. Potter in the garden. Pathetically small ambition, isn't it –

DIANA. Normal day?!

ROBIN. No drama.

DIANA. No, Robin, I'm afraid we can't have a normal day.

ROBIN. *(exhausted suddenly)* Oh God –

DIANA. Presumably you see why? Hmm? Or you don't think there's anything we need to discuss?

ROBIN. *(exiting)* I'm going to make some coffee.

DIANA. Nothing to do with us?

ROBIN. *(from the doorway)* Would you like one?

DIANA. No you're quite right. Course you are.

ROBIN. No?

DIANA. Nothing to see here, officer. Move along. Tinkle, tinkle.

(**ROBIN** *is offstage now. He says something inaudible.*)

(*Silence.*)

(**DIANA** *has a desolate quality suddenly.*)

(**ROBIN** *reappears gingerly.*)

ROBIN. In all seriousness, *would* you like me to make you a coffee?

DIANA. It's not alright, Robin.

ROBIN. Oh please –

DIANA. You must be capable of seeing that. Even you.

ROBIN. I don't know what you're talking about.

(**DIANA.** *laughs. Then, suddenly serious.*)

DIANA. Oh God you really don't, do you?

ROBIN. I've put the kettle on –

DIANA. But then this is why you can't trust the philistines to run the country, isn't it? You don't even understand what you're doing. It would be funny if it wasn't so frightening.

ROBIN. I'm not going to ask again.

DIANA. No capacity to understand how other people experience the world, that's the trouble.

(**ROBIN** *gives up and exits again.*)

No desire to, even –

ROBIN. *(offstage)* I'm going to take that as a yes.

DIANA. You know why? It's because you don't read.

I'm not wrong, you know –

ROBIN. *(offstage)* You never are, my love.

DIANA. Go on – when did you last read a novel?

ROBIN. A novel? *(appearing at the door – highly doubtful)* Really?

DIANA. Really.

ROBIN. Alright. I read that Jeffrey Archer over Easter –

DIANA. Jeffrey Archer doesn't count –

ROBIN. I'll tell him you said that.

DIANA. Because you know what it does? Fiction. It gives you a pattern.

ROBIN. *(mock sincere)* Does it really?

DIANA. Cause and effect. Otherwise it's too easy to let yourselves off the hook. Isn't it? If you never force yourself to understand the consequences of your actions –

ROBIN. No that's very good, dear –

DIANA. I'll do you a reading list. That's the answer. You could hand them out at cabinet. A bit of Margaret Drabble.

ROBIN. Excellent –

DIANA. Slip Virginia Woolf into Margaret's red box. That'll shake her up.

(**ROBIN.** *turns back to make his [instant] coffee.*)

ROBIN. No it's a terriffic idea. We'll start a book club! Everyone'll be thrilled –

DIANA. Or you could take them to the theatre.

ROBIN. The theatre?

DIANA. Cabinet outing –

ROBIN. Oh no, darling, no –

DIANA. Take Margaret to *Hedda Gabbler* – could change the whole course of British history.

(**ROBIN** *is suddenly on his safest ground.*)

ROBIN. Shall I tell you why we don't read your novels, Diana. Why we don't go to your plays.

DIANA. Because you'd have to engage with another point of view –

ROBIN. Because they're full of people like you.

DIANA. Sorry?

ROBIN. People with a vivid emotional life. People with a fine appreciation of beauty –

DIANA. No –

ROBIN. Well come on – it's never people with jobs, is it? Never people making roads, building companies, paying tax, is it? In these appalling plays you've taken me to. It's always the people who in real life contribute the absolute least who get all the sympathy. It's always the neurasthenic daughters, the artistic sons, the women –

DIANA. Sorry?

ROBIN. That's always where the sympathy resides –

DIANA. (*under her breath*) Did you say *the women*?

ROBIN. Oh I meet them in the green rooms. These liberal arts people, with their jumpers and their beards and their profound moments of epiphany, who don't have a clue about running the country. And yet somehow because they've read the latest Ian McKellen novel they think they can look down on those of us who are doing all these appalling oppressive things like worrying about employment figures and exchange rates and –

(**DIANA** *tries to interrupt.* **ROBIN** *doesn't let her.*)

No! You listen to me. You think your *culture* makes people empathetic. Open minded – that's your point isn't it? Well let me tell you, there is no group of people more intolerant than your theatre goers. More prejudiced and supercilious and convinced of their own rectitude. You try being a member of Margaret Thatcher's government and standing in the foyer of a theatre. If you wanted to talk about prejudice. If you want to talk about a lack of empathy.

(**DIANA** *is trying to hold off but she can't.*)

DIANA. Ian McEwan.

ROBIN. What?

DIANA. It doesn't matter –

ROBIN. Look at this week. These appalling people attacking the newsreaders. Disrupting the business of the House of Lords. If you're talking about the passing of the Local Government Act, which I think in your own inimitable way, you are.

Did you see how they behaved?

It's too much. The derangement of these people on the left. The feeling they have that the people who disagree with them are not only wrong but actually malevolent.

The result of which, of course, is that they are unable to engage with questions of policy in any reasonable way.

Because you know what it is? This section twenty eight they're up in arms about? It's a safeguarding measure.

DIANA. It's not a safeguarding measure. It's a deterrent –

ROBIN. Have you seen the books these councils are putting into schools? Young Gay and Proud. Honestly. Jenny Lives With Eric and Martin. Terrifying what they're doing to young people. They won't rest until we're all gay, or black, or at the very least disabled. I tell you in twenty years one won't be allowed to be a white heterosexual male. It'll be illegal.

DIANA. One can hope...

DIANA. Oh I see – you're worried it'll catch on, are you?

ROBIN. Sorry?

DIANA. One positive word from the headmaster and the entire sixth form will all have their hands down each others trousers –

ROBIN. No –

DIANA. But then this is the great anxiety of you public school men. Isn't it? That you might all be queer if you're not careful.

ROBIN. It's an incredibly delicate thing. Childhood.

DIANA. Yes, Robin, that's the point –

ROBIN. You can't go around telling children they can be whatever they want to be in life! Do whatever they want. Honestly.

*(Beat – **ROBIN** can't resist…)*

This isn't America.

*(This makes **ROBIN** chuckle).*

DIANA. Look at you. There's no inner life in there at all. Is there?

ROBIN. Not much, darling, no. You'll find as a conservative it's easier that way.

(Dazzling smile.)

Enables one to trample more cheerfully on the poor and needy –

DIANA. But then I suppose that's always been your template hasn't it?

ROBIN. Sorry?

DIANA. Don't mention the disaster and it doesn't exist.

I remember the first time I saw it in action, I was agog. That first summer with your family. Well it was my first exposure to the English upper class wasn't it? My God – I'd never *seen* so much well-dressed unhappiness. Because there wasn't just one elephant in the room. There were *herds* of them. The illegitimate child, the unmentionable sister, the sheer volume of heroin addiction among the nephews and nieces. And none of them so much as mentioned. I remember standing there watching you all, tinkling away as though nothing was happening –

ROBIN. Yes I'd rather you didn't start on my family again –

DIANA. Tinkle, tinkle –

ROBIN. I've done a coffee for you over here.

DIANA. As it all crashed down around you.

ROBIN. I SAID I'VE MADE YOU A COFFEE.

(*Beat.*)

And she wasn't a heroin addict. Arabella. She was at art school.

(*This makes* **ROBIN** *chuckle.*)

DIANA. You know when I realised what it was going to be like. That first day we got back from the hospital.

ROBIN. Sorry?

DIANA. She was here when we got back. Do you remember? Your mother. Inspecting the grandson. And we all came and sat in here and I remember I had him in my arms. And I was kissing him and telling him how much I loved him and how beautiful he was, and he was making those little dinosaur noises he made at the beginning, do you remember? And you see, naively, I had thought that everything was going to be alright now that the baby was here.

And then I looked up, and there was your mother.

She was watching me, and she had this tight little smile on her face.

You're very affectionate with him, aren't you, she said.

It's very sweet.

ROBIN. Well she wasn't sentimental –

DIANA. And I had the awful realization, suddenly, that this was just going to be another thing I was going to get wrong. Wasn't it? Motherhood.

ROBIN. She was a different generation –

DIANA. She thought I gave away my upbringing –

ROBIN. It wasn't that –

DIANA. Of course it was. It was always that.

ROBIN. It was about molly-coddling –

DIANA. It'll all end in tears. That's what she used to say to me. Did you know that? When nobody else could hear. She'd say it under her breath as she was walking past me. All end in tears, she'd say. *Such* a lovely woman –

ROBIN. Oh stop it, Di –

DIANA. But then she wasn't wrong, was she –

ROBIN. I said stop. You're determined to have a fight, but I don't want to have one.

DIANA. Oh dear, I'm sorry to hear that –

ROBIN. Not today –

> (**ROBIN.** *is striding over to the table to get something from a box underneath it.*)

DIANA. No, that's really rotten luck, Robin. Because I'm afraid we're already under way –

ROBIN. Oh God –

> (**ROBIN** *is muttering as he pulls out a box.*)

DIANA. I know! Show's already started, darling. No escape now. And you know the worst thing? There's no interval –

> (**ROBIN** *has found what he was looking for. It's an old megaphone from his canvassing days.*)

ROBIN. BE NICE TO ME!

DIANA. Be nice to you?

ROBIN. *(through the megaphone)* IT'S MY BIRTHDAY.

> *(Beat.)*

DIANA. It's your... it's not!

> (**DIANA** *thinks for a moment.*)

Oh my God it is!

(As though appalled.)

Well that *snuck* up on us...

ROBIN. *(with dignity)* I accept that we're beyond mawkish devotion, but I wonder if you might try not be on your most monstrous form. We could do Christmas Day on the Somme couldn't we? Go on. Emerge from our trenches. Stumble towards one another across the mud? Just for the day. I'll even be the Germans if you like?

*(**ROBIN** darts out and returns with a bottle of gin, which he places on the table.)*

Peace offering.

Please.

*(**ROBIN** exits again. From offstage we hear:)*

Singing softly.
STILLE NACHT! HEILIGE NACHT!
ALLES SCHLÄFT ...
...EINSAM WACHT.

(Silence.)

*(**ROBIN** reappears in the doorway. He looks at **DIANA**.)*

I often think. I've often thought. That we shouldn't have stopped doing a tree. At Christmas.

That that was a mistake.

*(**DIANA** is calm, forensic now.)*

DIANA. I don't want a fight, Robin.

ROBIN. Sorry?

DIANA. I want to be terribly calm, actually. Because I'm aware that if an argument is made in emotional terms – and particularly if that argument is made by a woman – then you're spared the obligation of engaging with it.

ROBIN. I don't understand.

DIANA. We'll start with *acceptability*, I think. Because that's a pretty paltry thing. Isn't it? To take away from the bewildered adolescent.

The local authority shall not promote the *acceptability* of homosexuality –

ROBIN. No don't get yourself into a state, darling –

DIANA. I'm not getting myself into a state –

ROBIN. The fact is, it's a very specific piece of legislation designed to protect children at a particularly vulnerable moment in their lives.

DIANA. No, Robin, no. It's a very specific piece of legislation designed to cement the support of the seventy-five percent of the British electorate who think that homosexuality is morally wrong.

ROBIN. *(very patiently)* No –

DIANA. But then that's always been the great talent of the right hasn't it? The ability to disguise craven electoral self-interest as the taking of a moral stand –

ROBIN. Yes, I'm afraid it was in the manifesto.

DIANA. Sorry?

ROBIN. I know! Isn't that a bore. Blame the people, darling – they voted for us –

DIANA. Oh don't worry, I do blame the British people. Can't trust them with anything important –

ROBIN. *(laughing)* Terrible habit of getting it wrong?

DIANA. But then of course they do, when you lot are out there, pandering to their worst instincts.

ROBIN. Oh I know… we are simply *awful* aren't we. Catching the mood of the electorate like that –

DIANA. You don't catch the mood of the electorate, Robin. You create it.

ROBIN. Is that right?

DIANA. You teach them what to want. And then you promise to give it to them –

ROBIN. My God, it's like spending the day with Noam Chomsky –

DIANA. It's not funny –

ROBIN. No, but listen, if you want to blame someone, blame the Labour Party. All their fault!

DIANA. What do you mean?

ROBIN. Look at them. If they will keep choosing the most unappealing people possible as their leaders, then this is what is going to happen. We're going to be in power forever.

DIANA. Don't change the subject –

ROBIN. We watch them over the dispatch box and we can't believe our luck. The succession of badly dressed geography teachers they march out in front of us.

DIANA. I see you, Robin. I've been watching it for thirty years. You make people feel that something is under attack. The nation state, the family, the Falkland Islands – and then you promise to defend it –

ROBIN. The Falkland Islands *were* under attack –

DIANA. But the trouble with your model is that you have to generate an enemy all the time.

(*If* **ROBIN**'s *near it, he might say this through the megaphone.*)

ROBIN. THEY LANDED AT PORT STANLEY –

DIANA. There always has to be a threat. Doesn't there? That's the equation. Some demonised group against which you turn people –

ROBIN. Oh dear, no, I see what's happened. You've been at *The Guardian* again, haven't you?

DIANA. No –

ROBIN. We've talked about this, Diana. It's terribly dangerous. It's why I keep telling them in the village shop not to sell it to you. Terrifying combination of righteous indignation and typographical inaccuracy –

DIANA. You know what's dangerous, Robin? You are. This breed of yours –

ROBIN. No, darling, I'm not going to do it. I'm sorry.

(ROBIN holds up his hand to prevent her interjection.)

I used to be willing to put up with these rows when they were a necessary part of our sex life but I'm afraid the appeal of debating the issues of the day with you has abated somewhat of late – oh my God, unless – *(gasp of realisation)*

DIANA. What?

ROBIN. She's not going to get her *allure* out again is she? Holy shit, she is! That's why you're not dressed! You thought we might rekindle the dying embers, did you? Bring the conjugal soot pan back to life? And why not? We used to be quite good at it, didn't we? Back in the day.

Get some cod liver oil in me, who knows what I'll be capable of. A spoonful of malt and I shall be ravishing you on the stairs. What do you say?

DIANA. I say you want to be careful, Robin.

(Beat.)

Because one can feel quite destructive. Sitting out here in this house. Listening to you all on the radio. And I keep having this thought, you see, that perhaps I've got a duty to do something about it. Blow the whistle, as it were.

ROBIN. Blow what whistle?

DIANA. I mean I suppose I could drive into Oxford, couldn't I? Walk into the BBC building on the Banbury Road. Say I've got a bit of background they might be interested in.

Take the old cine film with me. *They'd* watch it! I mean, I see it would be bad form, talking to the press. But then I never did know how to behave, did I? Barely knew how to hold my knife when we first met. Like a pencil. Do you remember? You used to wince. And as for the bringing up of children – my God – total embarrassment!

ROBIN. I don't know what this game is, but I'm telling you now, I don't want to play –

DIANA. Yes, I'm afraid it's going to have to be a new one today.

(Beat. Eye contact.)

You show me your shame, I'll show you mine. That's the gist of it.

ROBIN. *(laughing)* Gosh, isn't that rotten luck. Because I'm afraid I'm off games today – note from matron and everything –

DIANA. Think of it as a sort of confession –

ROBIN. Sorry?

DIANA. Bad form notwithstanding.

ROBIN. Confession?

DIANA. That's it.

*(Silence. Then, exaggerated, as though **ROBIN***'s blood has run cold.)*

ROBIN. Oh my God –

DIANA. Fraid so, Robin –

ROBIN. So it was you! How could you, Diana! My own wife!

DIANA. What are you doing?

ROBIN. And there I was, all these months, thinking it was the fox. I can see you now, out there with the trowel while I'm up in London. Just turning up the dial on my blood pressure? Is that the idea? Hastening the arrival of the long promised coronary?

DIANA. That's it.

ROBIN. You brute! Don't think I haven't spotted you trying to get my cholesterol up.

DIANA. Tinkle tinkle.

ROBIN. I saw you last weekend, slipping an extra yolk in my scrambled egg.

DIANA. Tinkle away.

ROBIN. Poor me, honestly! And yet still I come back to be abused by you like this. Week after week I flog my way through the Hanger Lane gyratory. The Oxford bypass! Year after year. Oh Christ, I've just had a terrible realization! You know what it must be? Why I come back?

(horror-struck) I must still love you!

(**ROBIN.** *turns and leaves.*)

(offstage) Terrifying thought…

DIANA. Don't you dare do that. Not today.

(**DIANA** *gets up and goes over to her bag. She takes out a battered-looking exercise book. She puts it on the table.*)

(**DIANA** *is facing away from the door.* **ROBIN** *reappears and watches her. He has gone to get a battered and faded old silk hankerchief, which he will tie around his neck and tuck into his collar.*

ROBIN. *(he has dropped the play-acting tone)* It might be true, you know.

It might be love.

It might be longing.

(**ROBIN** *has also brought* **DIANA**'*s dress down with him.*)

Anyway… I brought this down.

(**ROBIN** *lays it over the back of the chair or hangs it on the back of the door.*)

It's twenty past twelve, Di. Might you consider getting dressed?

DIANA. *(quietly)* I came up to the flat.

ROBIN. I'm sorry?

DIANA. On Wednesday.

ROBIN. But I wasn't there on Wednesday.

(**DIANA** *turns back to* **ROBIN**.)

Oh I see.

DIANA. Rotten luck, wasn't it –

ROBIN. Well you should have said –

DIANA. Yes –

ROBIN. You should have warned me –

DIANA. But it wasn't planned, you see. One minute I was sitting here, listening to your colleagues talking about safeguards on the radio. Next thing I know, I'm in the mini metro, hurtling up Stokenchurch hill. Suddenly realised I had to do it, you see –

ROBIN. But you haven't come up to the flat for years.

DIANA. I know!

ROBIN. I don't think you've *ever* come up without telling me –

DIANA. Unbearable, isn't it? But then, how was I to know it was Wednesdays. Because it used to be a Thursday in our day, didn't it? During the reign of my predecessor –

ROBIN. What did you want?

DIANA. Oh come on, Robin. There were one or two things we might have discussed, do you not think? I know it's not the house style, but I'm beginning to feel it might not have stood us in the most brilliant stead. I mean I still remember your mother keeping her appointment at the hairdresser the next day –

ROBIN. What are you doing?

DIANA. *This Is Your Life.* That's the game. I'll play Michael Aspel, you play you.

ROBIN. I don't –

DIANA. My God I remember that moment vividly. That Nofolk house. There she was. Full make up, hand bag, one of her little suits. Walking though the hall. What are you doing, I say.

I'm going for my rince, she replies.

(**ROBIN** *looks horrified.*)

I know! That's the look I gave her. Christ, I thought, there's a woman who knows how to brush a catastrophe under the carpet.

(**ROBIN** *looks at* **DIANA**. *She is glittering with emotion. Suddenly, he becomes very hard. Nasty.*)

ROBIN. Well there we are, you'll know for next time.

DIANA. Sorry?

ROBIN. Not to come up to the flat like that.

ROBIN. Because I'd hate for you to be disappointed like that again.

And it can be a terribly busy day, a Wednesday.

DIANA. Can it?

ROBIN. Chockablock. One thing after another. But then this is what happens when one's as devoted to one's constituents as I am.

DIANA. Is that right?

ROBIN. Tireless I am. Indefatigable.

DIANA. How long have you been devoted to them in this tireless manner?

ROBIN. Oh years, Diana. Years and years. All along.

Speaking of which, I don't suppose you listened, did you?

DIANA. Sorry?

ROBIN. Last night? Don't suppose you found time in your exhausting schedule for that?

DIANA. Listened?

ROBIN. It was my *Any Questions?*, Diana. Live from Leeds. No? No of course you didn't. But then it's a lot to ask, isn't it? Actually to have to think about somebody else for a moment. Stupid of me. Imagine having the gumption to hope that ones wife might be interested enough to put down her gin and stagger across to the wireless. Ridiculous. I always forget that you're the only person who exists in your universe. That every event that ever happens in the world is actually about you.

(*Beat.* **ROBIN** *recovers his poise.*)

Anyway... You'll be thrilled to hear that your beloved emerged more or less unscathed. One or two smatterings of applause, even.

DIANA. Did you really?

ROBIN. Apparently the PM listened from Chequers.

DIANA. No!

ROBIN. Apparently.

(**ROBIN** *settles. He has swerved the conversation away from danger.*)

Word is, I shall be getting a little pat on the head on Monday.

DIANA. Not a *pat on the head*!

ROBIN. It's not an easy thing, *Any Questions?*.

DIANA. Or the bottom, do you think?

ROBIN. What?

DIANA. Does she do pats on the bottom, Margaret? When you've really stuck it to em –

ROBIN. No –

DIANA. I bet she does if you're Alan Clark. Cecil –

ROBIN. Not even then –

DIANA. Oh I don't know, Robin. I see the way she straightens all your ties – picks the fluff of your lapels. She's like a dominant female gorilla.

ROBIN. She really isn't –

DIANA. Prowling her pack –

ROBIN. I promise you –

DIANA. All these men, panting up at her with your willies throbbing away in your Y-fronts –

ROBIN. For goodness sake –

DIANA. Oh my God it's not her is it?

ROBIN. Sorry?

DIANA. The Wednesdays? Because that really would be something – if it was Margaret you were whisking away to Wolverhampton –

ROBIN. She's Mummy.

DIANA. I'm sorry?

ROBIN. The straightening of ties.

DIANA. *Mummy?*

ROBIN. The fluff on the lapel.

DIANA. Oh that really is heartbreaking –

ROBIN. I'm saying she's a profoundly un-erotic woman.

DIANA. Darling, I know your mother was more or less the missing link between Nancy Mitford and Attila the Hun. But the point about Mummy, in general, is that she's the soppy one. Do you see? Mummy's the one you turn to when you need a bit of a cuddle. And I'm not sure that's the *first* thing I think of when I look at Margaret. Christ – I don't even imagine Carol gets much of a squeeze.

ROBIN. She's the Prime Minister, Diana. She's not Esther Rantzen.

DIANA. I wonder if there's a psychological explanation for it. Maybe she had an appalling experience of childbirth. Maybe one of them got stuck on the way out –

ROBIN. Must be it –

DIANA. Do you think?

ROBIN. If only they'd been quicker with the forceps –

DIANA. Well it's either that or she's got one of the syndromes, isn't it? What's the one called where you're unable to imagine the impact of your actions on somebody else?

ROBIN. It's called Free Market Economics.

DIANA. I'm not joking.

ROBIN. Oh cheer up, darling. You can have a Bloody Mary soon. That'll take the edge off. Crush a couple of your valium in.

(**ROBIN** *laughs.* **DIANA** *surveys him. She is full of sincere emotion suddenly.*)

DIANA. You don't, though. Do you?

ROBIN. Don't what?

DIANA. Imagine what it might be like. And I do believe that's a failing. You think I'm sentimental and unserious and naive and that I don't understand how politics works. But look at your bill, Robin. Look at what it really means. Because I thought the first principle was the duty of care? Is that not right? Do no harm?

ROBIN. Oh God, I'm really going to have to do this am I?

DIANA. Do what?

(**ROBIN** *puts the lemon and the knife down.*)

ROBIN. Imagine two sets of parents, darling.

DIANA. Right.

ROBIN. And both these sets of parents are teaching their child how to ride a bicycle. First set are terribly protective. Every time their child falls off, they rush over and scoop him up. Ask him where it hurts, kiss it better. Horrid old bike, they say, throwing you off like that. In the end they can't bear it any more and they screw the stabilisers back on. That'll keep you safe, they say –

DIANA. Yes I'm just about there –

ROBIN. Meanwhile, the second set of parents take a different approach –

DIANA. *(as though amazed)* They *don't* –

ROBIN. The point is they don't love their child any less than the first set of parents. They also hate to see him hurt himself. They also want to rush straight over and re-attach the stabilisers. But they resist this urge. Instead they force themselves to appear nonchalant, relaxed. Come on old boy, they say, up you get –

DIANA. No that's very good, darling –

ROBIN. But you see my point –

DIANA. No I do. As a woman I find a domestic analogy *such* a help...

ROBIN. The point is you have to ask yourself which set of parents are being kinder. Actually. To the child –

DIANA. No, it's these difficult decisions you always talk about –

ROBIN. Yes exactly –

DIANA. Tory Party prides itself on taking –

ROBIN. One wants the boy to be on his BMX, Diana. That's all I'm trying to say. Zooming off down the hill with his friends.

(**ROBIN.** *resumes the Bloody Mary making.*)

One wants him to thrive.

(**DIANA** *nods, allowing* **ROBIN** *to feel that she has seen the wisdom of his argument.*)

DIANA. No, you know why it's so brilliant? Your analogy.

ROBIN. Because there's more than one way to *mind* about people.

(Beat.)

DIANA. Because you're always standing up there at the top of the hill.

ROBIN. *(ambushed)* Sorry?

DIANA. No – as a visual representation of the relationship between the Conservative Party and the people they govern, it's got it all –

ROBIN. Oh don't be so aggravating –

DIANA. Because it's always somebody else who's clattering onto the tarmac. Isn't it? It's always the miners or the social workers or the fledgling homosexuals who are being carted off to hospital –

ROBIN. *(laughing)* Oh my God, she's going to start on the miners!

DIANA. Nothing's ever going to touch you –

ROBIN. But then this is the classic intellectual cowardice of the left, isn't it? So much easier to argue against a distortion of who we are –

DIANA. I'm not distorting anything –

ROBIN. Shall I tell you a secret about the miners – and I hate to spoil your story, but the Conservative Party isn't killing off the mining industry. It's dying all on it's own.

(It's a good Bloody Mary he's making. Celery salt, lemon juice, sherry, vodka...)

And you know what? That's a bloody good thing. Because it's dangerous and it's polluting and it's an awful way to make a living. Isn't it? Stuck in a hole in the ground, clogging up their lungs? Lousy pay? No prospect of advancement? And do you think young people want to do these jobs? Of course they don't. They want to get out, Diana! They want to buy a bigger television and a new car and they want to own their own home –

DIANA. Oh you're doing them a *favour*!

ROBIN. They want *more*!

DIANA. Of course!

ROBIN. And you know what they don't want? To be pitied by people like you, who romanticise the working-class way of life without having a clue about it. Because you know what it does? That attitude. It keeps people in their place.

So don't talk to me about the miners. And don't talk to me about Margaret either. As though she was sitting there in Downing Street plotting the destruction of the working poor. Honestly. You preach empathy at me but somehow you never think it's encumbent on you to understand Margaret, do you? Well I hate to break it to you, but she's not Pol Pot!

DIANA. No?

ROBIN. She's not even General Pinochet –

DIANA. Oh I don't know, darling. I saw her, sticking out of that tank...

ROBIN. *(slowly, patiently)* Yes, if you'd listen, rather than attacking me, you'd discover that I am explaining something to you.

DIANA. How incredibly unusual.

ROBIN. No relationship with her mother.

DIANA. Sorry?

ROBIN. That's the key to understanding Margaret Thatcher.

DIANA. I don't –

ROBIN. Ask Margaret about her mother. Nothing. You saw that interview on the television. She couldn't think of one thing to say about her, could she? Look at her Who's Who. She doesn't mention her once. Daughter of the late Alfred Roberts.

Full stop. That's who Margaret is. No Mummy. No cuddles, or whatever you think she ought to be giving Carol.

DIANA. I don't understand your point.

ROBIN. My point is that we're all formed out of our own experience. Aren't we? That's how Margaret has been formed. She's strong because she wasn't looked after. Because she wasn't molly coddled. As a result, that's how she thinks you make other people strong. She thinks: don't *look after* people if you want them to do well. Don't encourage failure by subsidising it. Do you see?

You think like the Labour Party. You think that if somebody is weak what they need is protection. Looking after. Special status. Wrong. Worst thing to do. That's what Margaret sees. That's why people don't like her. They want a her to be sentimental.

DIANA. They want her to be human, that's all –

ROBIN. She's a bloody difficult woman, I accept that. She's not a normal person. She's got no real personality, actually. No sense of humour. She's a nightmare to sit next to at dinner. All of that. But she's not a monster, Diana.

*(By this stage **ROBIN** has finished the Bloody Mary, tasted it, added more celery salt, more pepper, and finally decided it is perfect.)*

(He has crossed to the fridge to put it in there. He opens the fridge door as he is talking.)

And you know what else she isn't?

(*The fridge is open but he hasn't looked into it yet.*)

A bottom patter.

(*He laughs. Finally he looks down into the fridge.*)

Oh no!

DIANA. What?

(**ROBIN** *looks up at her, desolate.*)

ROBIN. I can't bear it!

DIANA. What?

ROBIN. You've forgotten the Scotts are coming!

DIANA. No I haven't –

ROBIN. And you've got a plan for lunch have you?

DIANA. For lunch?

(**ROBIN** *lavishly demonstrates the emptiness of the fridge to her. He is furious.*)

ROBIN. Only the fridge is looking particularly Soviet this morning, even by your standards.

(*As though with a sudden lurch of horror.*)

DIANA. But I thought you were doing lunch –

ROBIN. What do you mean?

DIANA. I thought it was your turn –

ROBIN. My turn?

DIANA. Was that not right?

ROBIN. But it hasn't been my turn once in thirty years!

(**DIANA** *smiles at him.*)

Oh very funny.

DIANA. I just gave you the rope, darling.

ROBIN. You've been rubbing away at Germaine Greer again, have you?

DIANA. That's it –

ROBIN. No listen, I'd be thrilled if you discovered feminism. I would. Only I'm afraid the boring thing about emancipating yourself from the shackles of the weekly shop is that you have to do something else in its place.

DIANA. Is that right?

ROBIN. Look at you! Sitting here in your nightie. And it's not that much to ask is it? A bit of cold ham. Some coronation chicken. I work bloody hard, Diana. And nobody else has to put up with this sort of performance. Do they? Even the Tebbits can manage a Sunday lunch, and she's paralysed from the neck down.

DIANA. Oh don't –

ROBIN. This is what it's come down to. Isn't it? This is what our life has dwindled to. My birthday lunch and the only item fit for consumption in the entire house is one small slab of cheddar – My God.

(Beat.)

DIANA. Yarg.

ROBIN. What?

DIANA. As opposed to cheddar.

ROBIN. It's not a Yarg! Well that changes everything! And how might you serve up this great Cornish treat? Cold on crackers? Was that the plan? Or were you going to stretch all the way to cheese on toast?

DIANA. I find if you call it a rarebit –

ROBIN. Oh do you –

DIANA. Smear of mustard, you know –

ROBIN. Excellent.

DIANA. Anyway. I shouldn't worry too much about the Scotts. They're like all our friends over sixty. They're only eating to soak up the claret.

(**ROBIN** *laughs and, as he does so, he almost loses his breath.
He might have to hold onto something to steady himself.
It lasts a moment and then it passes.*)

(*He finds himself looking at the long dining table with its
mess and its boxes. He feels about a hundred years old.*)

ROBIN. Twelve at a squeeze...

DIANA. I'm sorry?

ROBIN. Ten comfortably, twelve at a squeeze.

First thing we ever bought together, wasn't it. You and I. As
a pair. Antique shop in Woodstock.

Ridiculous, of course. This enormous table for the two of us,
but the man persuaded us it was the thing we most needed
in the world. Do you remember?

You'll live your life around a table like that. That was his pitch.
Birthdays, clan gatherings, long Sunday lunches stretching
into the afternoon. By the time he'd finished talking we were
almost worried it was too small. Thirty pounds it cost. Absolute
fortune.

Funny the things that stay with you, isn't it. Vast swathes
of ones life get washed away and these moments remain.
Absolutely intact.

Pair of suckers, I suppose.

But then one had such confidence, didn't one. In the shape
one's life would have. Ability to make it happen.

(*This is an appeal to her...*)

When we embarked on all this.

(*Beat.*)

DIANA. She's got a well stocked fridge, has she?

ROBIN. Sorry?

DIANA. Wednesday nights.

ROBIN. Oh Di, don't –

DIANA. Nursery food, I imagine? Steamed puddings. Tapioca? That sort of thing –

(Suddenly, a loud awful scream comes from the garden. They both freeze.)

ROBIN. What was that?

(Another scream. After a moment:)

My God. It's not the fox?

(They both cross to the window.)

Sounds like someone's being murdered out there.

(Another scream. They stand and look out. Horrified.)

DIANA. You know what it's doing, don't you?

ROBIN. You're going to tell me it's mating –

DIANA. It's summoning its friends!

ROBIN. Oh don't!

(Another scream from outside.)

DIANA. From the Welsh valleys, they will come...

*(**ROBIN** goes to look. Opens the window, shouts out at them.)*

ROBIN. Do you know who I am?

I'm on the agriculture and fisheries select committee. I could order a cull!

*(Then, back to **DIANA**.)*

And you know what's going to happen next? They'll be coming through this Channel Tunnel.

(Beat.)

DIANA. Not foreign foxes!

ROBIN. It's serious.

DIANA. It's unbearable! They think they can just come in here, eat our hens, ravage our lawns –

ROBIN. You laugh but they're saying we'll have someone there with a gun when it breaks through, shooting them as they come out.

DIANA. That's what she wants is it?

ROBIN. Because of what they'll bring in –

DIANA. Yes –

ROBIN. All the things we've been safe from as an island.

DIANA. No it's brilliant, darling, because I suspect they'll be lacking the moral values too.

ROBIN. Sorry?

DIANA. Honestly – blast *I Vow To Thee My Country* out into the garden and you've got a re-run of the manifesto. No wonder you frighten them all into voting for you.

ROBIN. Oh you want rabies back in the country do you?

DIANA. Sorry?

ROBIN. Well exactly! Honestly.

And we don't frighten people into voting for us.

DIANA. Of course you do. You work out which particular subset of the population they're most prejudiced against and you're off.

ROBIN. There we are! You wanted to know why people keep putting us back in power?

DIANA. Sorry?

ROBIN. That's why. Because you mistake people's legitimate concerns for prejudice. And you know what – funnily enough, people don't like being called bigots. You'd be amazed –

DIANA. But it's always us against them. Isn't it? That's always the story you tell –

ROBIN. That's what politics *is*, Diana. Us against them. That's literally how it works. And people need to have a story. They need to be told who they are. Always have. George and the Dragon. Henry the Fifth. It's a human need. We'll fight them on the beaches –

DIANA. We'll arrest them at the ports!

ROBIN. I'm sorry?

DIANA. We'll find them on the ferries.

ROBIN. No! So you did listen to *Any Questions?*.

DIANA. Of course I listened. I'm your wife.

ROBIN. And?

What did you think?

DIANA. What did I think?

(Beat. With sadness.)

I was unbelievably ashamed of you.

(Beat.)

ROBIN. You didn't agree with Polly Toynbee?

DIANA. I thought she was very persuasive –

ROBIN. I'd be persuasive if I was a liberal in a large house in Islington –

DIANA. She was being kind!

ROBIN. I hate to tell you, but politics isn't just about being kind to people –

DIANA. Although I suppose that wouldn't be a bad place to start.

ROBIN. Anyway, I'm not going to go into all this.

*(**ROBIN** gets up and moves across to the table.)*

We'll take them out to the pub, will we?

DIANA. I'm sorry?

ROBIN. The Scotts. Given the absence of food in the house. We'll tell them you've had a frantic week. Torrid time at the hairdressers.

(He gets out the phone book from a desk drawer.)

I'll book a table – meanwhile, do you think you might manage to get dressed? It might give a slightly more normal air to proceedings. Or are we going to tell them you were too busy for that as well?

*(Suddenly he notices **DIANA** is opening the notebook she put on the table earlier.)*

DIANA. We could start with the Thesaurus story, I suppose.

ROBIN. The what?

DIANA. You remember the Thesaurus story, Robin. Twelve children sitting in a circle on the floor. It's a birthday party and there's an entertainer. Smarty Arty, he's called. And he goes round the room and he asks all the children what their favourite dinosaurs are, and all the other children say the Diplodocus or the Pterodactyl or the Tyrannosaurus. Until it comes to the birthday boy and he sits there, very solemnly, very seriously, and he says the Thesaurus is his favourite dinosaur.

And all the grown ups laughed – you remember – and he didn't know why it was funny – and he burst into tears and he came and sat on his mother's knee – and his father said – well, come on – what did his father say? Right in front of all of his friends?

ROBIN. What are you doing?

DIANA. We all need a story. That was what you said, wasn't it? Otherwise how do we know who we are? George and the Dragon. Don't be such a girl about it. That's what you said. By the way.

*(**DIANA** is turning the pages of the exercise book now.)*

ROBIN. What's that?

DIANA. As luck would have it, you see.

(reading) "June 17th, 1973. Dad took me out for lunch. <u>Lot</u> of material today", he's written. Lot underlined. "We went to the dreaded club."

ROBIN. That's not –

DIANA. I know! Isn't that tremendous. At least one of us kept a record. Because I tell you, it's all here. Story after story.

"Dad ordered a bottle of claret and we ate enormous and extremely manly steaks. After lunch he said, I've got a birthday present for you." –

"We got in the car, and he drove us down to a mews off the Bayswater Road. We got out and he rang a door bell. Have fun, he said. I'll be parked round the corner."

ROBIN. This is in unbelievably bad taste –

DIANA. Linda, her name was. She said, I hear it's someone's birthday.

"In the car on the way back to school, Dad asked me how it had been. She was a knock out I said. I let him drive on for a bit, looking pleased with me. Then I said: the thing is, we shared an absolute abhorrence for chintz. You shared what? Chinz, I said. Neither of us can stand it. I tell you, she's got a real eye for fabric." –

ROBIN. That's enough now –

DIANA. "You should go and have a look, I said. Her curtains are a fabulous Toile de Jouy."

(**DIANA** *looks up at* **ROBIN**. *Brutal.*)

Coming back to you, is it?

Because it's all there, Robin. Our own private Hansard.

And there's masses more, if you'd like it. I tell you he's bloody good.

ROBIN. What are you doing?

DIANA. The boy on the bicycle. Seeing as that's the analogy we're using. Wobbling down the road. The parents watching on. I brought it down with me. On Wednesday. I thought we might have a read of it together. Before the vote, you see –

ROBIN. Do you want to know where I was on Wednesday?

DIANA. Not really –

ROBIN. Where do you think I was?

DIANA. It doesn't even matter –

ROBIN. No go on – tell me.

Beat.

DIANA. I rang through to Barabara in the office.

"Are you having a lovely time?" she said. "What a treat for you both to get away mid-week." –

ROBIN. I can explain if you want me to –

DIANA. I'd like you to know I pulled it off. Oh yes, I said. Huge treat.

ROBIN. It's not what you think.

DIANA. It's not? Oh God – it's not love, is it?

ROBIN. Love?

DIANA. I mean sex, I think one could cope with. But what if it was some nice middle-aged woman in an alice band. That would be the real killer. Corduroy skirt. Sensible shoes –

ROBIN. Do you want me to explain or not?

DIANA. If there was no sex at all! If you just clambered into bed. Read each other tit bits from *The Times*.

ROBIN. You've misunderstood –

DIANA. You didn't come back all night.

ROBIN. You didn't stay all night?

DIANA. I sat on the chair by the door, waiting to hear your footsteps on the stairs. Only they never came. Did they?

ROBIN. No.

DIANA. But you made it to the vote, though, did you? From wherever it was you were? Yes of course you did.

(**DIANA** *looks at* **ROBIN**. *Then, quietly.*)

How could you, Robin?

And then to go out on the radio and defend it.

Why didn't you tell them that it couldn't be you they sent out. Of all the people in the government.

ROBIN. I wanted to do it.

DIANA. You *wanted* to?

ROBIN. You still don't see it.

DIANA. It's hate, Robin. That's what it is.

ROBIN. No –

DIANA. Of course it is. You say they're unacceptable and you give permisssion to people to hate them. You encourage it.

ROBIN. You misunderstand –

DIANA. But you can imagine what it's like for the child. Can you? Some frightened boy, discovering who he is. Going to a teacher to ask for help. Because, just to be clear: not only does this bill tell that teacher that it would be illegal – *illegal* – to tell the bewildered quivvering child in front of her that everything is going to be alright. It also tells that child that all his worst anxieties are true. That he is unacceptable –

ROBIN. And you'd like them to be told it's going to be a walk in the park would you? To be a homosexual? That your big idea?

DIANA. I'd like them to be told it's normal –

ROBIN. But it's not the norm, Di. That's the point. And it's not an easy life. If one lived in... San Francisco maybe it would be different. But we don't. This is England. We're a conservative nation. We are. People want to be part of a community that resembles them. They want to know who they are. They want the world to look more or less like it did when they were growing up and they felt safe. And before you start, that's not prejudice, that's human nature. People trust other people who are like them. Ask a black man. Ask him who he would trust his life to. Ask the Pakistanis in Bradford. Ask the Sikhs in Hounslow.

DIANA. Yes, that's the feeling you exploit, Robin –

ROBIN. No –

DIANA. Of course you do. You identify it and then you exploit it –

ROBIN. I'm saying it's easier to be in the majority. In life. I'm saying that you want to let a young person choose the life that will offer the most. Open every door for them.

DIANA. It's only easier if that's who you are –

ROBIN. One's not fully formed at that age, Diana. Still malleable. And it's not a bad thing, to be sent off in an easier direction. Because it does shut you out from things, Diana. That sort of life. You can't deny that. Family. Children. Power, actually, if that's important to you.

And there's a sadness to it. I think there is. A loneliness. Look at cousin John. Sitting there in that house on his own. Surrounded by all that china. And I see them – you don't – but I do. Standing there at the urinal in the public loos. It's not a full life, Diana.

You think the best thing is to tell them their life is going to be wonderful. But perhaps it isn't. Perhaps it's going to be bloody difficult.

And this AIDS, Diana. If you saw them.

DIANA. Sorry?

ROBIN. These young men. Wasting away –

DIANA. *(white hot anger, suddenly)* Don't you dare. Don't you *dare* do that. When you have been using that illness to demonise them –

ROBIN. That's not what we've done –

DIANA. Look at your newspapers, Robin! A plague. That's what they call it. If you want to know how frightening it is to realise when you're fifteen-years-old that that's how you happen to fall in love –

ROBIN. Oh for goodness sake, you really think we're all bigoted, do you? Is that it? Grow up, Diana. The party is full of homosexuals. Look at St John-Stevas –

DIANA. Oh no I don't think you're bigoted. It's worse than that. I think you're cynical. And I think you're careless. That's the really unforgivable thing.

I don't think you've given them a second thought, the bewildered young person coming to terms with who they are. I think that they're just collateral damage in your desire to be elected. To be in power. That's what's really disgusting.

You all talk endlessly about morality in the Tory Party but let me tell you, I can think of no act more profoundly immoral than taking away from a young person the help that they are asking for.

Because you know what that is? This silence you are inflicting on the teacher. On the child? It's a death sentence. And for you, Robin. For you, of all people, to be out there, defending this thing. Talking about a duty of care –

ROBIN. That's enough –

DIANA. Because I think it would have made a difference. Don't you? To the way people heard you last night. If they'd known that the man out there on the radio talking about safeguards. Talking about a duty of care, had a son all of his own.

Swam out one day into the Norfolk broads.

ROBIN. What are you doing?

DIANA. Sunny day, Robin. Cloudless sky.

ROBIN. No thank you –

DIANA. Because it wasn't an accident sort of day, was it?

Not a ripple on the water.

And how many times had we all swum there? The three of us. Over all those summers.

ROBIN. That's enough now –

DIANA. "Died suddenly". That's what you and your mother had them put in *The Times*. "Died suddenly while on holiday."

And then on the Monday morning you went back up to London and we never spoke about him again. Did we? Not really. Not in any meaningful way.

I mean I know that's how your family always operated but it's quite something, Robin, isn't it? When you think about it. Not to have discussed the central fact of our existence.

Worst thing is that it's a way of keeping a person alive. Talking about them. And not to have even done him that honour –

ROBIN. I don't think you want to do this –

DIANA. And I know you had a quiet word with someone. Didn't you? Kept it out of the papers. Off the coroner's report. No need for it to become a story.

Well you'd just got your seat. And a thing like that can really follow you around. The fact that we had failed, the two of us, at the one thing that really matters in this life. Can really hamper a career –

ROBIN. For Christ's sake, Diana, it was for you!

DIANA. What was?

ROBIN. "Died suddenly".

DIANA. I don't understand –

ROBIN. For once in your life. For *once* in your life. Take responsibility for something will you?

Because you think it went well? Your version of looking after? Do you? All that emotion you shoveled into him? You think that turned out well in the end?

And if we didn't talk about it, if I did have a quiet word with someone, can you possibly imagine that it might have been for your sake?

But this is what you always do, isn't it? You let yourself off the hook. Well, enough, Diana. Enough. You tell me how dangerous I am. But take a look at yourself. Everything you've ever done has gone bad. Hasn't it? Everything you've ever touched. No wonder nobody comes near you.

Have you ever stopped to ask yourself why that is? Because I'm the only person here, aren't I? I'm the only person who comes anywhere near you.

In return for which, I wonder if you might possibly do me the courtesy of going and getting your FUCKING CLOTHES ON.

(**ROBIN***'s last explosion of rage. He throws something or knocks something to the ground. It smashes.*)

(*Long silence.*)

DIANA. Right.

ROBIN. I didn't mean –

DIANA. That's what you think went wrong.

ROBIN. I just want you to get dressed. That's all. The Scotts'll be here in a minute.

DIANA. The over-loving mother.

ROBIN. Please don't be like this when they come.

DIANA. You think you were protecting me from that.

ROBIN. Please. It's important to me.

(Beat.)

DIANA. Yes. I needed to be zipped up.

ROBIN. I'm sorry?

DIANA. That's why I'm not dressed.

Because I needed someone to help me.

Stuck out here on my own. Nobody comes anywhere near me.

*(**DIANA** exits to get her dress, which is hanging up on the back of a door somewhere close by.)*

(In the hallway, she takes off her dressing gown. She is wearing a slip.)

(She steps into her dress.)

ROBIN. You make a choice, Di. The kind of life you want to have.

This is what I chose.

This life we had. That we squandered.

A family. A house like this. Children running through the kitchen, playing in the garden.

*(**DIANA** is standing at the door now.)*

I remember standing at the window showing him. When he was a baby.

One day, my boy, all this will be yours. *(He is laughing at himself)* Pathetic. Ridiculous. Quarter of an acre outside Burford.

You wonder why I mind about my stupid lawn? That's why. Because it was for him. Because I was making this perfect wicket for him. Back and forward with the roller. All that first summer.

Perfect cricket pitch. On which I thought I would bowl and bowl and bowl at him – at my son – I would keep going until the middle of the night if that was what he wanted.

Always have enough time. Opposite of my father.

Only it was never what he wanted.

Always far away from me.

Never...friends.

DIANA. He was sixteen.

ROBIN. He didn't like me.

DIANA. It would have changed.

ROBIN. And the two of you. I did worry about it. You knew that. All that emotion between you.

(**DIANA** *walks towards* **ROBIN**. *Lifts up her hair, turns so that he can zip up her dress.*)

I'm not trying to blame you.

It's all my mother was ever trying to say too. I know she didn't express it well. You have to prepare a child for the world as it really is. Not how you wish it was.

DIANA. I'd been out all morning running errands.

ROBIN. Sorry?

DIANA. At lunchtime I came home. As I said I would.

ROBIN. I don't –

DIANA. Sunny day, Robin. Cloudless sky.

(*Silence.*)

That house. The lawn stretching down to the water.

I called up the stairs.

Tom, I said. I'm home

No answer. Which was strange. Because normally he would have bounded down to me, wouldn't he?

Halfway up the stairs I called out again. Still no answer. And then I heard a floorboard creaking in our bedroom.

It wasn't til I got to the threshold of our room that I saw him.

And now of course I realise that he looked incredibly beautiful. Heart-stoppingly beautiful. Actually. Our son, standing in the window of our bedroom with the sun pouring in on him.

(Silence.)

ROBIN. You mean –

DIANA. I mean there was nothing sordid about it. I think that's the most important thing for me to say.

That there was something pure about it. Actually.

Not to do with sex.

But to do with who he was.

In fact I think in some way he probably looked more himself than he had ever looked before.

ROBIN. I don't understand.

DIANA. It was my going away dress from our wedding. Do you remember? That fine grey silk. My God I'm proud of him. When I think of the bravery of that moment.

ROBIN. Alright –

DIANA. Because I should say before I go on that he knew that I was coming home for lunch. Which means of course that this moment was a deliberate unveiling. Do you see? He was asking for my help, Robin.

And for a moment I stood there in the threshold of our room, not knowing what to do. And he looked at me. At his Mum. Who had, as you say, always been his ally and his friend. Always encouraged him to be himself. He looked at me, and he smiled. "Hello Mum", he said. And he held out his hands to me.

And so you see I have to hope it was the shock.

ROBIN. I'm sorry?

DIANA. Panic. If I'm being kind to myself.

That I'd somehow done this to him. As you always said I would. As your mother said I would that first day we came home from the hospital. The over-loving mother. The sensitive boy.

ROBIN. I don't understand –

DIANA. And perhaps I can take your line. Perhaps I felt a sadness. Mourning. In that split second. For the things that wouldn't be available to him. The children he wouldn't have.

Possibly. If I'm charitable to myself about that brief moment in which life asked something of me, and in which I failed.

Because I'm afraid that what I have to confront. What I have to come to terms with. Is the fact that perhaps I was disgusted.

Do you see?

Perhaps I was repulsed.

Perhaps that was what I felt when I saw my beautiful boy, my brilliant boy, standing in my bedroom, asking me for help.

With my rouge on his cheeks and that first hair that had just appeared on his chest –

ROBIN. I don't need to know any more –

DIANA. Oh but you do, Robin. Because you can see how much faith he had in me in that moment. Can't you? That I would do the right thing. That I was the person he could rely on. Because we know what I ought to have said. Don't we? To my boy. Standing there in my dress. All of his life stretching out ahead of him. I ought to have told him that I loved him, oughtn't I?

ROBIN. What happened?

DIANA. Told him everything was going to be OK. That he was going to have the best life. The fullest life. That he would find a tribe of people in which he would belong. That I would accept him, that you would, that if people didn't, that was their problem and not his.

ROBIN. What happened?

DIANA. Oh Robin, I didn't say any of those things.

Not any of them.

ROBIN. What happened?

(Silence.)

DIANA. I slapped him.

I slapped him in the face.

My boy, who I loved more than any other thing I'd ever known. Who I had carried in my womb. Who was asking me for help. Who was my whole life.

(Silence.)

ROBIN. It wasn't that day?

(They stare at one another.)

DIANA. I sat on the stairs, waiting for him to come back. All that afternoon, into the evening. Waiting for him to walk through the door.

It was nearly midnight when I heard footsteps coming up the path. Oh thank God, I thought.

Only of course... when I opened the door... police woman.

Diana Heskth, she said.

(Silence.)

And she took off her hat.

(Silence.)

I never got the chance to say sorry. To tell him how much I loved him.

*(**ROBIN** watches her. He sits, taking in everything he has just learned.)*

ROBIN. Why didn't you tell me?

(Silence.)

You should have told me.

(Silence.)

DIANA. You could have left me if I'd told you.

(Silence.)

ROBIN. I could have looked after you.

DIANA. Oh don't say that.

ROBIN. I could have tried.

(Silence.)

DIANA. And then this bill. You see? To see it all happen again.

ROBIN. No –

DIANA. It's the same mistake, Robin. It is.

It would have made a difference. On Wednesday. Wouldn't it?

If I'd been brave enough to tell you. If you'd been there to hear.

*(**ROBIN** looks at **DIANA**. Bewildered.)*

That was the last time I ever saw him. His cheek red where I had hit him.

(Long silence.)

*(**DIANA** is standing, crumpled. **ROBIN** is staring at her. He wants to reach out to touch her, but he can't.)*

ROBIN. I was in Norfolk.

On Wednesday.

That's where I was.

(Silence.)

DIANA. I don't understand.

ROBIN. He was my son too, Di.

DIANA. You go there?

ROBIN. Sometimes.

DIANA. Why didn't you tell me?

ROBIN. It's been... private.

(They look at each other. Long silence.)

DIANA. So you weren't...

ROBIN. No of course I wasn't.

*(Silence. **DIANA** sits down.)*

(tender, desolate) There's never been anyone else, you stupid woman.

Just you.

(If he cries, it is as he says his son's name.)

You and Tom.

(Silence. It looks as though they might reach out for each other. They don't.)

Anyway. Scotts'll be here in a minute.

*(**ROBIN** shakes his head to stop her. He begins to get the room ready.)*

(When he reaches the cine projector, he turns it on.)

(Blazing into life comes Tom.)

(The film is silent but he is chatting and cartwheeling and laughing. He is wonderful.)

(It doesn't last long. Ten seconds, fifteen maybe.)

*(The camera pans from Tom to **DIANA**. She is laughing too. She is luminously happy.)*

And then it ends, the reel flickering loose and the square of light on the wall of their room bright and empty. If the moment can sustain, then the longer it flickers an empty square, the sound of the projector loud in the darkness, the better.

*(**DIANA** turns the projector off.)*

He knew, Di. He knew how much you loved him.

(The faint sound of car on gravel.)

*(**ROBIN** begins to wind up the extension lead. **DIANA** is holding the plug. He is moving slowly towards her as he winds.)*

We'll take them to the pub.

DIANA. What?

ROBIN. *(Kindly.)* It doesn't matter. It's not important.

　(Silence. They are close but not facing each other.)

DIANA. She's bringing lunch.

　Claire.

　She's made a coronation chicken.

　*(**DIANA** goes into one of the kitchen cupboards).*

　(She turns. She is holding a birthday cake in her hands.)

　(She is the saddest woman in the world.)

　Happy Birthday.

　(Silence.)

ROBIN. He would have thrived. Wouldn't he?

DIANA. Yes. Yes he would.

　(Silence.)

ROBIN. The waste.

DIANA. Yes.

ROBIN. All of it.

　(They walk towards one another.)

　(A few steps apart they stop.)

　(Silence.)

　(As they are about to reach out and hold each other, the lights go down, and they are gone.)

ABOUT THE AUTHOR

Simon Woods studied English Literature at Oxford University. *Hansard* is his first play as a writer. As an actor his work in TV includes *Rome, Cranford, Spooks*. Film includes *Pride and Prejudice, Penelope* and *Starter for 10*.

Milton Keynes UK
Ingram Content Group UK Ltd.
UKHW021843190924
448478UK00010B/185

9 780573 132